Note From Creator:

During my experience as a law student, BAR stud BAR tutor and law school professor, time and time again I came across students who are bombarded with so much material and information that they could not help but become overwhelmed and anxious, which prevents students from performing at their best potential.

I created Legal E. Noted workbooks as a tool to help you take your resources and materials to the point of understanding what you need to take away from them. By completing the sections within your Legal E. Written workbook, you will be left with just the right amount of information you need to study for your exam. By the end of your course, if you have followed the advice given and completed your workbook pages accordingly, after all the lectures, briefs, and study materials have been utilized, your Legal E. Noted workbooks will guide you on the minimal information you actually need for your midterm and finals as opposed to piles of endless material (sigh of relief!!).

Not only will Legal E. Noted workbooks lighten your load, the habits developed will prove that digesting the information this way will enlighten your mind! These practices will prove so useful when it comes to bar study where there will not be case briefs to hold on to – just rules. But that's okay because you'll be ready!

I know some of you may want a PDF version of your Legal E. Noted workbooks because you are accustomed to typing your class notes. However, studies have shown there is an undeniable advantage, resulting in increased scores on exams, for those who handwrite notes in class. Still, the conciseness of Legal E. Noted methods is compatible enough to allowing you the flexibility to type notes and still have time to handwrite the information required in your Legal E. Noted workbook, giving you the opportunity to experience the benefits of both worlds!

Please review the steps indicated on the "How To Use Your Legal E. Noted Workbook" page. The way your notes will translate into your exams is by your using the information as follows:

After having read the exam fact pattern and determining which rule you will be applying in your analysis of the facts, remember to include the various extensions of the rule where applicable. Having had distinguished the various parts in your notes will help you remember just how many parts there are. Also, at times it may be difficult to create an argument for both parties, the plaintiff vs. defendant or prosecution vs. defendant. However, this is where the court's reasoning may help you with ideas on formulating the appropriate argument. For example, if a defendant has a clear argument in their favor and it seems the plaintiff does not have an argument against it, think about why the extensions of the rule exist (court's reasoning) and take another look into the facts to find a way to help the plaintiff's argument. If there is not an argument, sometimes simply recognizing and informing the reader that such an argument does not exist in the fact pattern as it is written it will give you the opportunity for extra points!!

You just may find yourself having fun with your analysis now that your Legal E. Noted workbook helps you streamline your material into clearer opportunities for POINTS!

– E. Harrell

How To Use Your Legal E. Noted Workbook:

In class, with a Legal E. Noted workbook at your side, complete the course topic, and subtopic information along with the date and week number of your class. Circle whether or not the particular page marks the beinning of the topic or if it's a continuation from the previous page. Same for the subtopic.

Then, complete a short case name in the space provided. Circle whether or not the case being briefed is an extension of the subtopic being discussed (see example: first section "N" circled because it is the first case on the subtopic of false imprisonment; however, following case sections circle "Y" because those cases elaborate on how to analyze the elements of the same subtopic of false imprisonment).

Next, during your class lecture, the "point/purpose/reasoning" of each case assigned will be discussed along with the established rule/exception/standard/definition set by the case ruling. Once you have an understanding of the information reviewed and discussed, fill-in the sections provided for the case reasoning and rule prior to moving on to the next case. If you struggle formulating the reasoning or the rule sections of your Legal E. Noted workbook for a particular case, this is a good indication you will struggle to analyze the information in an exam fact pattern. At this point, you should seek other resources to find and understand the information, i.e., speaking to your professor for clairification.

The "Exam Point(er)s" area is a space that will draw your attention to the information that you absolutely do not want to forget. For instance, if your professor repeatedly stated a certain word or phrase when discussing a particular case, your professor may love to see those exact words or phrases used in the analysis of your exam (buzzwords) and that equals POINTS in your favor! You could also use the "Exam Point(er)s" section to save acronyms or other personal key information that is helpful to you in memorizing the rule or understanding when the rule should be applied for exam purposes.

Lastly, during any point in your quarter or semester, when or if your professor informs your class what will be on the exam, MARK THE BOX "to be tested!" AND, **for the love of law school,** MARK the boxes to all cases that are an extension of the general rule and study those as well! Your Legal E. Noted workbook will assist you in avoiding the common bad habit of missing points on your class exam or on the BAR exam because of simply analyzing the rule without its various additional components.

- Happy Studies!

EXAM POINT(er)S

BUZZ WORDS

or

KEY TERMS

CASE: City vs. State

Extension of Previous: Y (N) TO BE TESTED [X]

COURT'S Point/Purpose/Reasoning :	Rule (elements/definition ONLY) :
	First case in a topic will typically offer
EXAMPLES:	the general elements of a particular rule.
to eliminate...	Example: False Imprisonment Elements
to prevent...	1. act of restraint
to ensure....	2. confining plaintiff
to allow...	3. to bounded area
	4. intent to confine plaintiff

EXAM POINT(er)S

o NOT apply here ... !

CASE: Him vs. Her

Extension of Previous: (Y) N TO BE TESTED [X]

COURT'S Point/Purpose/Reasoning :	Rule (elements/definition ONLY) :
** Be sure to AVOID re-briefing	A following case may provide a
the case here. Refer to your case brief if	standard or definition to an element
need be BUT limit THIS space to	referenced above.
assisting yourself in understanding how and	Example: Element # 2 "confining plaintiff"
when to apply the related rule in your	Plaintiff must be AWARE
upcoming exam fact pattern.	of confinement or harmed

EXAM POINT(er)S

OK for ...

CASE: Jane Doe Case

Extension of Previous: (Y) N TO BE TESTED [X]

COURT'S Point/Purpose/Reasoning :	Rule (elements/definitions ONLY) :
	Next case may provide a standard or
	definition to a different element
	referenced above.
	Example: Element # 3 "bounded area"
	NOT bounded if REASONABLE means of
	escape & REASONABLY discoverable

Extension of Previous: (Y) N TO BE TESTED [X]

	Rule (elements/definitions ONLY) :
	Next case may provide an EXCEPTION
	to the elements referenced above.
	Example: Element # 3 ... re: escape ...
	any disgusting, dangerous or difficult
	means of escape
	NOT REASONABLE!

** IMPORTANT **

If the general rule is going to be tested, mark its box **AND ALL OTHER BOXES TO THE CASES THAT ARE AN EXTENSION OF THE RULE** because the extensions of the rule will more than likely be tested as well! This is where many students miss the opportunity to increase their score!! (unless otherwise instructed by your professor!!!!)

SUBJECT: _____

WEEK # _____

DATE _____

TOPIC: _____

SUBTOPIC: _____

BEGINNING / CONTINUED

BEGINNING / CONTINUED

EXAM POINT(er)S

CASE:

Extension of Previous: Y N   TO BE TESTED [

COURT'S Point/Purpose/Reasoning :	Rule (elements/definition ONLY) :

EXAM POINT(er)S

CASE:

Extension of Previous: Y N   TO BE TESTED [

COURT'S Point/Purpose/Reasoning :	Rule (elements/definition ONLY) :

EXAM POINT(er)S

CASE:

Extension of Previous: Y N   TO BE TESTED [

COURT'S Point/Purpose/Reasoning :	Rule (elements/definitions ONLY) :

EXAM POINT(er)S

CASE:

Extension of Previous: Y N   TO BE TESTED [

COURT'S Point/Purpose/Reasoning :	Rule (elements/definitions ONLY) :

SUBJECT: _____

TOPIC: _____

SUBTOPIC: _____

BEGINNING / CONTINUED

BEGINNING / CONTINUED

EXAM POINT(er)S

CASE:

Extension of Previous: Y N   TO BE TESTED ☐

COURT'S Point/Purpose/Reasoning :	Rule (elements/definition ONLY) :

EXAM POINT(er)S

CASE:

Extension of Previous: Y N   TO BE TESTED ☐

COURT'S Point/Purpose/Reasoning :	Rule (elements/definition ONLY) :

EXAM POINT(er)S

CASE:

Extension of Previous: Y N   TO BE TESTED ☐

COURT'S Point/Purpose/Reasoning :	Rule (elements/definitions ONLY) :

EXAM POINT(er)S

CASE:

Extension of Previous: Y N   TO BE TESTED ☐

COURT'S Point/Purpose/Reasoning :	Rule (elements/definitions ONLY) :

SUBJECT: _____ WEEK # _____

DATE _____

TOPIC: _____

SUBTOPIC: _____

BEGINNING / CONTINUED

BEGINNING / CONTINUED

EXAM POINT(er)S

CASE: _____ Extension of Previous: Y TO BE
                                                   N TESTED [

COURT'S Point/Purpose/Reasoning :	Rule (elements/definition ONLY) :

EXAM POINT(er)S

CASE: _____ Extension of Previous: Y TO BE
                                                   N TESTED [

COURT'S Point/Purpose/Reasoning :	Rule (elements/definition ONLY) :

EXAM POINT(er)S

CASE: _____ Extension of Previous: Y TO BE
                                                   N TESTED [

COURT'S Point/Purpose/Reasoning :	Rule (elements/definitions ONLY) :

EXAM POINT(er)S

CASE: _____ Extension of Previous: Y TO BE
                                                   N TESTED [

COURT'S Point/Purpose/Reasoning :	Rule (elements/definitions ONLY) :

L e g a l E . N o t e d

SUBJECT: _____ DATE _____ WEEK # _____

TOPIC: _____ SUBTOPIC: _____

BEGINNING / CONTINUED   BEGINNING / CONTINUED

EXAM POINT(er)S   CASE: _____   Extension of Previous: Y N   TO BE TESTED ☐

COURT'S Point/Purpose/Reasoning :	Rule (elements/definition ONLY) :

EXAM POINT(er)S   CASE: _____   Extension of Previous: Y N   TO BE TESTED ☐

COURT'S Point/Purpose/Reasoning :	Rule (elements/definition ONLY) :

EXAM POINT(er)S   CASE: _____   Extension of Previous: Y N   TO BE TESTED ☐

COURT'S Point/Purpose/Reasoning :	Rule (elements/definitions ONLY) :

EXAM POINT(er)S   CASE: _____   Extension of Previous: Y N   TO BE TESTED ☐

COURT'S Point/Purpose/Reasoning :	Rule (elements/definitions ONLY) :

Legal E. Noted

EXAM POINT(er)S   CASE: _____   Extension of Previous: Y / N   TO BE TESTED ☐

COURT'S Point/Purpose/Reasoning :	Rule (elements/definition ONLY) :

EXAM POINT(er)S   CASE: _____   Extension of Previous: Y / N   TO BE TESTED ☐

COURT'S Point/Purpose/Reasoning :	Rule (elements/definition ONLY) :

EXAM POINT(er)S   CASE: _____   Extension of Previous: Y / N   TO BE TESTED ☐

COURT'S Point/Purpose/Reasoning :	Rule (elements/definitions ONLY) :

EXAM POINT(er)S   CASE: _____   Extension of Previous: Y / N   TO BE TESTED ☐

COURT'S Point/Purpose/Reasoning :	Rule (elements/definitions ONLY) :

SUBJECT: _____

TOPIC: _____

SUBTOPIC: _____

BEGINNING / CONTINUED

BEGINNING / CONTINUED

EXAM POINT(er)S

CASE: _____

Extension of Previous: Y N   TO BE TESTED ☐

COURT'S Point/Purpose/Reasoning :	Rule (elements/definition ONLY) :

EXAM POINT(er)S

CASE: _____

Extension of Previous: Y N   TO BE TESTED ☐

COURT'S Point/Purpose/Reasoning :	Rule (elements/definition ONLY) :

EXAM POINT(er)S

CASE: _____

Extension of Previous: Y N   TO BE TESTED ☐

COURT'S Point/Purpose/Reasoning :	Rule (elements/definitions ONLY) :

EXAM POINT(er)S

CASE: _____

Extension of Previous: Y N   TO BE TESTED ☐

COURT'S Point/Purpose/Reasoning :	Rule (elements/definitions ONLY) :

SUBJECT: _____   WEEK # _____

DATE _____

TOPIC: _____

BEGINNING / CONTINUED

SUBTOPIC: _____

BEGINNING / CONTINUED

EXAM POINT(er)S

CASE: _____   Extension of Previous: Y N   TO BE TESTED ⌐

COURT'S Point/Purpose/Reasoning :	Rule (elements/definition ONLY) :

EXAM POINT(er)S

CASE: _____   Extension of Previous: Y N   TO BE TESTED ⌐

COURT'S Point/Purpose/Reasoning :	Rule (elements/definition ONLY) :

EXAM POINT(er)S

CASE: _____   Extension of Previous: Y N   TO BE TESTED ⌐

COURT'S Point/Purpose/Reasoning :	Rule (elements/definitions ONLY) :

EXAM POINT(er)S

CASE: _____   Extension of Previous: Y N   TO BE TESTED ⌐

COURT'S Point/Purpose/Reasoning :	Rule (elements/definitions ONLY) :

SUBJECT: _____

WEEK # _____

DATE _____

TOPIC: _____

SUBTOPIC: _____

BEGINNING / CONTINUED

BEGINNING / CONTINUED

EXAM POINT(er)S

CASE: _____

Extension of Previous: Y N   TO BE TESTED ☐

COURT'S Point/Purpose/Reasoning :	Rule (elements/definition ONLY) :

EXAM POINT(er)S

CASE: _____

Extension of Previous: Y N   TO BE TESTED ☐

COURT'S Point/Purpose/Reasoning :	Rule (elements/definition ONLY) :

EXAM POINT(er)S

CASE: _____

Extension of Previous: Y N   TO BE TESTED ☐

COURT'S Point/Purpose/Reasoning :	Rule (elements/definitions ONLY) :

EXAM POINT(er)S

CASE: _____

Extension of Previous: Y N   TO BE TESTED ☐

COURT'S Point/Purpose/Reasoning :	Rule (elements/definitions ONLY) :

EXAM POINT(er)S CASE: _____ Extension of Previous: Y N TO BE TESTED [

COURT'S Point/Purpose/Reasoning :	Rule (elements/definition ONLY) :

EXAM POINT(er)S CASE: _____ Extension of Previous: Y N TO BE TESTED [

COURT'S Point/Purpose/Reasoning :	Rule (elements/definition ONLY) :

EXAM POINT(er)S CASE: _____ Extension of Previous: Y N TO BE TESTED [

COURT'S Point/Purpose/Reasoning :	Rule (elements/definitions ONLY) :

EXAM POINT(er)S CASE: _____ Extension of Previous: Y N TO BE TESTED [

COURT'S Point/Purpose/Reasoning :	Rule (elements/definitions ONLY) :

SUBJECT: _____

WEEK # _____

DATE _____

TOPIC: _____

SUBTOPIC: _____

BEGINNING / CONTINUED

BEGINNING / CONTINUED

EXAM POINT(er)S   CASE: _____

Extension of Previous: Y N   TO BE TESTED ☐

COURT'S Point/Purpose/Reasoning :	Rule (elements/definition ONLY) :

EXAM POINT(er)S   CASE: _____

Extension of Previous: Y N   TO BE TESTED ☐

COURT'S Point/Purpose/Reasoning :	Rule (elements/definition ONLY) :

EXAM POINT(er)S   CASE: _____

Extension of Previous: Y N   TO BE TESTED ☐

COURT'S Point/Purpose/Reasoning :	Rule (elements/definitions ONLY) :

EXAM POINT(er)S   CASE: _____

Extension of Previous: Y N   TO BE TESTED ☐

COURT'S Point/Purpose/Reasoning :	Rule (elements/definitions ONLY) :

EXAM POINT(er)S   CASE: _____   Extension of Previous: Y   TO BE
                                                              N   TESTED [

COURT'S Point/Purpose/Reasoning :	Rule (elements/definition ONLY) :

EXAM POINT(er)S   CASE: _____   Extension of Previous: Y   TO BE
                                                              N   TESTED [

COURT'S Point/Purpose/Reasoning :	Rule (elements/definition ONLY) :

EXAM POINT(er)S   CASE: _____   Extension of Previous: Y   TO BE
                                                              N   TESTED [

COURT'S Point/Purpose/Reasoning :	Rule (elements/definitions ONLY) :

EXAM POINT(er)S   CASE: _____   Extension of Previous: Y   TO BE
                                                              N   TESTED [

COURT'S Point/Purpose/Reasoning :	Rule (elements/definitions ONLY) :

EXAM POINT(er)S   CASE: Extension of Previous: Y N   TO BE TESTED ☐

COURT'S Point/Purpose/Reasoning :	Rule (elements/definition ONLY) :

EXAM POINT(er)S   CASE: Extension of Previous: Y N   TO BE TESTED ☐

COURT'S Point/Purpose/Reasoning :	Rule (elements/definition ONLY) :

EXAM POINT(er)S   CASE: Extension of Previous: Y N   TO BE TESTED ☐

COURT'S Point/Purpose/Reasoning :	Rule (elements/definitions ONLY) :

EXAM POINT(er)S   CASE: Extension of Previous: Y N   TO BE TESTED ☐

COURT'S Point/Purpose/Reasoning :	Rule (elements/definitions ONLY) :

SUBJECT: _____ WEEK # _____

DATE _____

TOPIC: _____

SUBTOPIC: _____

BEGINNING / CONTINUED

BEGINNING / CONTINUED

EXAM POINT(er)S

CASE: _____ Extension of Previous: Y N TO BE TESTED ☐

COURT'S Point/Purpose/Reasoning :	Rule (elements/definition ONLY) :

EXAM POINT(er)S

CASE: _____ Extension of Previous: Y N TO BE TESTED ☐

COURT'S Point/Purpose/Reasoning :	Rule (elements/definition ONLY) :

EXAM POINT(er)S

CASE: _____ Extension of Previous: Y N TO BE TESTED ☐

COURT'S Point/Purpose/Reasoning :	Rule (elements/definitions ONLY) :

EXAM POINT(er)S

CASE: _____ Extension of Previous: Y N TO BE TESTED ☐

COURT'S Point/Purpose/Reasoning :	Rule (elements/definitions ONLY) :

SUBJECT: _____

WEEK # _____

DATE _____

TOPIC: _____

SUBTOPIC: _____

BEGINNING / CONTINUED

BEGINNING / CONTINUED

EXAM POINT(er)S CASE: _____

Extension of Previous: Y N   TO BE TESTED ☐

COURT'S Point/Purpose/Reasoning :	Rule (elements/definition ONLY) :

EXAM POINT(er)S CASE: _____

Extension of Previous: Y N   TO BE TESTED ☐

COURT'S Point/Purpose/Reasoning :	Rule (elements/definition ONLY) :

EXAM POINT(er)S CASE: _____

Extension of Previous: Y N   TO BE TESTED ☐

COURT'S Point/Purpose/Reasoning :	Rule (elements/definitions ONLY) :

EXAM POINT(er)S CASE: _____

Extension of Previous: Y N   TO BE TESTED ☐

COURT'S Point/Purpose/Reasoning :	Rule (elements/definitions ONLY) :

EXAM POINT(er)S   CASE: _____   Extension of Previous: Y N   TO BE TESTED [

COURT'S Point/Purpose/Reasoning :	Rule (elements/definition ONLY) :

EXAM POINT(er)S   CASE: _____   Extension of Previous: Y N   TO BE TESTED [

COURT'S Point/Purpose/Reasoning :	Rule (elements/definition ONLY) :

EXAM POINT(er)S   CASE: _____   Extension of Previous: Y N   TO BE TESTED [

COURT'S Point/Purpose/Reasoning :	Rule (elements/definitions ONLY) :

EXAM POINT(er)S   CASE: _____   Extension of Previous: Y N   TO BE TESTED [

COURT'S Point/Purpose/Reasoning :	Rule (elements/definitions ONLY) :

SUBJECT: _____ WEEK # _____

DATE _____

TOPIC: _____

SUBTOPIC: _____

BEGINNING / CONTINUED

BEGINNING / CONTINUED

EXAM POINT(er)S **CASE:**   Extension of Previous: Y N   TO BE TESTED ☐

COURT'S Point/Purpose/Reasoning :	Rule (elements/definition ONLY) :

EXAM POINT(er)S **CASE:**   Extension of Previous: Y N   TO BE TESTED ☐

COURT'S Point/Purpose/Reasoning :	Rule (elements/definition ONLY) :

EXAM POINT(er)S **CASE:**   Extension of Previous: Y N   TO BE TESTED ☐

COURT'S Point/Purpose/Reasoning :	Rule (elements/definitions ONLY) :

EXAM POINT(er)S **CASE:**   Extension of Previous: Y N   TO BE TESTED ☐

COURT'S Point/Purpose/Reasoning :	Rule (elements/definitions ONLY) :

L e g a l E . N o t e d

SUBJECT: _____

WEEK # _____

DATE _____

TOPIC: _____

SUBTOPIC: _____

BEGINNING / CONTINUED

BEGINNING / CONTINUED

EXAM POINT(er)S

CASE: _____

Extension of Previous: Y N   TO BE TESTED ☐

COURT'S Point/Purpose/Reasoning :	Rule (elements/definition ONLY) :

EXAM POINT(er)S

CASE: _____

Extension of Previous: Y N   TO BE TESTED ☐

COURT'S Point/Purpose/Reasoning :	Rule (elements/definition ONLY) :

EXAM POINT(er)S

CASE: _____

Extension of Previous: Y N   TO BE TESTED ☐

COURT'S Point/Purpose/Reasoning :	Rule (elements/definitions ONLY) :

EXAM POINT(er)S

CASE: _____

Extension of Previous: Y N   TO BE TESTED ☐

COURT'S Point/Purpose/Reasoning :	Rule (elements/definitions ONLY) :

EXAM POINT(er)S **CASE:** _____ Extension of Previous: Y N   TO BE TESTED ☐

COURT'S Point/Purpose/Reasoning :	Rule (elements/definition ONLY) :

EXAM POINT(er)S **CASE:** _____ Extension of Previous: Y N   TO BE TESTED ☐

COURT'S Point/Purpose/Reasoning :	Rule (elements/definition ONLY) :

EXAM POINT(er)S **CASE:** _____ Extension of Previous: Y N   TO BE TESTED ☐

COURT'S Point/Purpose/Reasoning :	Rule (elements/definitions ONLY) :

EXAM POINT(er)S **CASE:** _____ Extension of Previous: Y N   TO BE TESTED ☐

COURT'S Point/Purpose/Reasoning :	Rule (elements/definitions ONLY) :

SUBJECT: _____ DATE _____

TOPIC: _____

SUBTOPIC: _____

BEGINNING / CONTINUED   BEGINNING / CONTINUED

EXAM POINT(er)S   CASE: _____   Extension of Previous: Y N   TO BE TESTED ☐

COURT'S Point/Purpose/Reasoning :	Rule (elements/definition ONLY) :

EXAM POINT(er)S   CASE: _____   Extension of Previous: Y N   TO BE TESTED ☐

COURT'S Point/Purpose/Reasoning :	Rule (elements/definition ONLY) :

EXAM POINT(er)S   CASE: _____   Extension of Previous: Y N   TO BE TESTED ☐

COURT'S Point/Purpose/Reasoning :	Rule (elements/definitions ONLY) :

EXAM POINT(er)S   CASE: _____   Extension of Previous: Y N   TO BE TESTED ☐

COURT'S Point/Purpose/Reasoning :	Rule (elements/definitions ONLY) :

SUBJECT: _____ DATE _____

TOPIC: _____ SUBTOPIC: _____

BEGINNING / CONTINUED   BEGINNING / CONTINUED

EXAM POINT(er)S   **CASE:** _____   Extension of Previous: Y N   TO BE TESTED ☐

COURT'S Point/Purpose/Reasoning :	Rule (elements/definition ONLY) :

EXAM POINT(er)S   **CASE:** _____   Extension of Previous: Y N   TO BE TESTED ☐

COURT'S Point/Purpose/Reasoning :	Rule (elements/definition ONLY) :

EXAM POINT(er)S   **CASE:** _____   Extension of Previous: Y N   TO BE TESTED ☐

COURT'S Point/Purpose/Reasoning :	Rule (elements/definitions ONLY) :

EXAM POINT(er)S   **CASE:** _____   Extension of Previous: Y N   TO BE TESTED ☐

COURT'S Point/Purpose/Reasoning :	Rule (elements/definitions ONLY) :

SUBJECT: _____

WEEK #_____

DATE _____

TOPIC: _____

SUBTOPIC: _____

BEGINNING / CONTINUED

BEGINNING / CONTINUED

EXAM POINT(er)S

CASE: _____

Extension of Previous: Y N   TO BE TESTED [

COURT'S Point/Purpose/Reasoning :	Rule (elements/definition ONLY) :

EXAM POINT(er)S

CASE: _____

Extension of Previous: Y N   TO BE TESTED [

COURT'S Point/Purpose/Reasoning :	Rule (elements/definition ONLY) :

EXAM POINT(er)S

CASE: _____

Extension of Previous: Y N   TO BE TESTED [

COURT'S Point/Purpose/Reasoning :	Rule (elements/definitions ONLY) :

EXAM POINT(er)S

CASE: _____

Extension of Previous: Y N   TO BE TESTED [

COURT'S Point/Purpose/Reasoning :	Rule (elements/definitions ONLY) :

SUBJECT: _____

WEEK # _____

DATE _____

TOPIC: _____

SUBTOPIC: _____

BEGINNING / CONTINUED

BEGINNING / CONTINUED

EXAM
INT(er)S

CASE:

Extension of Previous: Y N   TO BE TESTED ☐

COURT'S Point/Purpose/Reasoning :	Rule (elements/definition ONLY) :

EXAM
INT(er)S

CASE:

Extension of Previous: Y N   TO BE TESTED ☐

COURT'S Point/Purpose/Reasoning :	Rule (elements/definition ONLY) :

EXAM
INT(er)S

CASE:

Extension of Previous: Y N   TO BE TESTED ☐

COURT'S Point/Purpose/Reasoning :	Rule (elements/definitions ONLY) :

EXAM
INT(er)S

CASE:

Extension of Previous: Y N   TO BE TESTED ☐

COURT'S Point/Purpose/Reasoning :	Rule (elements/definitions ONLY) :

SUBJECT: _____ DATE _____

TOPIC: _____

SUBTOPIC: _____

BEGINNING / CONTINUED   BEGINNING / CONTINUED

EXAM POINT(er)S   CASE: _____   Extension of Previous: Y N   TO BE TESTED

COURT'S Point/Purpose/Reasoning :	Rule (elements/definition ONLY) :

EXAM POINT(er)S   CASE: _____   Extension of Previous: Y N   TO BE TESTED

COURT'S Point/Purpose/Reasoning :	Rule (elements/definition ONLY) :

EXAM POINT(er)S   CASE: _____   Extension of Previous: Y N   TO BE TESTED

COURT'S Point/Purpose/Reasoning :	Rule (elements/definitions ONLY)

EXAM POINT(er)S   CASE: _____   Extension of Previous: Y N   TO BE TESTED

COURT'S Point/Purpose/Reasoning :	Rule (elements/definitions ONLY)

SUBJECT: _____ DATE _____

TOPIC: _____

SUBTOPIC: _____

BEGINNING / CONTINUED

BEGINNING / CONTINUED

EXAM POINT(er)S | ## CASE: _____ | Extension of Previous: Y / N | TO BE TESTED ☐

COURT'S Point/Purpose/Reasoning :	Rule (elements/definition ONLY) :

EXAM POINT(er)S | ## CASE: _____ | Extension of Previous: Y / N | TO BE TESTED ☐

COURT'S Point/Purpose/Reasoning :	Rule (elements/definition ONLY) :

EXAM POINT(er)S | ## CASE: _____ | Extension of Previous: Y / N | TO BE TESTED ☐

COURT'S Point/Purpose/Reasoning :	Rule (elements/definitions ONLY) :

EXAM POINT(er)S | ## CASE: _____ | Extension of Previous: Y / N | TO BE TESTED ☐

COURT'S Point/Purpose/Reasoning :	Rule (elements/definitions ONLY) :

SUBJECT: _____ DATE _____

TOPIC: _____ SUBTOPIC: _____

BEGINNING / CONTINUED   BEGINNING / CONTINUED

EXAM POINT(er)S   CASE: _____   Extension of Previous: Y   TO BE
                                                                   N   TESTED [

COURT'S Point/Purpose/Reasoning :	Rule (elements/definition ONLY) :

EXAM POINT(er)S   CASE: _____   Extension of Previous: Y   TO BE
                                                                   N   TESTED [

COURT'S Point/Purpose/Reasoning :	Rule (elements/definition ONLY) :

EXAM POINT(er)S   CASE: _____   Extension of Previous: Y   TO BE
                                                                   N   TESTED [

COURT'S Point/Purpose/Reasoning :	Rule (elements/definitions ONLY) :

EXAM POINT(er)S   CASE: _____   Extension of Previous: Y   TO BE
                                                                   N   TESTED [

COURT'S Point/Purpose/Reasoning :	Rule (elements/definitions ONLY) :

SUBJECT: _____ DATE _____

TOPIC: _____ SUBTOPIC: _____

BEGINNING / CONTINUED   BEGINNING / CONTINUED

EXAM POINT(er)S **CASE:**   Extension of Previous: Y N   TO BE TESTED ☐

COURT'S Point/Purpose/Reasoning :	Rule (elements/definition ONLY) :

EXAM POINT(er)S **CASE:**   Extension of Previous: Y N   TO BE TESTED ☐

COURT'S Point/Purpose/Reasoning :	Rule (elements/definition ONLY) :

EXAM POINT(er)S **CASE:**   Extension of Previous: Y N   TO BE TESTED ☐

COURT'S Point/Purpose/Reasoning :	Rule (elements/definitions ONLY) :

EXAM POINT(er)S **CASE:**   Extension of Previous: Y N   TO BE TESTED ☐

COURT'S Point/Purpose/Reasoning :	Rule (elements/definitions ONLY) :

SUBJECT: _____

WEEK # _____

DATE _____

TOPIC: _____

SUBTOPIC: _____

BEGINNING / CONTINUED

BEGINNING / CONTINUED

EXAM POINT(er)S   CASE: _____   Extension of Previous: Y N   TO BE TESTED ☐

COURT'S Point/Purpose/Reasoning :	Rule (elements/definition ONLY) :

EXAM POINT(er)S   CASE: _____   Extension of Previous: Y N   TO BE TESTED ☐

COURT'S Point/Purpose/Reasoning :	Rule (elements/definition ONLY) :

EXAM POINT(er)S   CASE: _____   Extension of Previous: Y N   TO BE TESTED ☐

COURT'S Point/Purpose/Reasoning :	Rule (elements/definitions ONLY) :

EXAM POINT(er)S   CASE: _____   Extension of Previous: Y N   TO BE TESTED ☐

COURT'S Point/Purpose/Reasoning :	Rule (elements/definitions ONLY) :

SUBJECT: _____ DATE _____

TOPIC: _____

SUBTOPIC: _____

BEGINNING / CONTINUED

BEGINNING / CONTINUED

EXAM INT(er)S

CASE: _____

Extension of Previous: Y N   TO BE TESTED ☐

COURT'S Point/Purpose/Reasoning :	Rule (elements/definition ONLY) :

EXAM INT(er)S

CASE: _____

Extension of Previous: Y N   TO BE TESTED ☐

COURT'S Point/Purpose/Reasoning :	Rule (elements/definition ONLY) :

EXAM INT(er)S

CASE: _____

Extension of Previous: Y N   TO BE TESTED ☐

COURT'S Point/Purpose/Reasoning :	Rule (elements/definitions ONLY) :

EXAM INT(er)S

CASE: _____

Extension of Previous: Y N   TO BE TESTED ☐

COURT'S Point/Purpose/Reasoning :	Rule (elements/definitions ONLY) :

TOPIC: _____ SUBTOPIC: _____

BEGINNING / CONTINUED   BEGINNING / CONTINUED

EXAM POINT(er)S   CASE: _____   Extension of Previous: Y N   TO BE TESTED

COURT'S Point/Purpose/Reasoning :	Rule (elements/definition ONLY) :

EXAM POINT(er)S   CASE: _____   Extension of Previous: Y N   TO BE TESTED

COURT'S Point/Purpose/Reasoning :	Rule (elements/definition ONLY) :

EXAM POINT(er)S   CASE: _____   Extension of Previous: Y N   TO BE TESTED

COURT'S Point/Purpose/Reasoning :	Rule (elements/definitions ONLY)

EXAM POINT(er)S   CASE: _____   Extension of Previous: Y N   TO BE TESTED

COURT'S Point/Purpose/Reasoning :	Rule (elements/definitions ONLY)